Original title:
Martian Madrigals

Copyright © 2025 Creative Arts Management OÜ
All rights reserved.

Author: Charles Whitfield
ISBN HARDBACK: 978-1-80567-803-8
ISBN PAPERBACK: 978-1-80567-924-0

Odes to the Organs of Oblivion

In the dust of red rocks, a squeaky gasp,
A ticklish tale of a giggling rasp.
An alien's sneeze makes the moon jump high,
While robots laugh, and the stars blink sly.

Wobbly creatures dance, with legs of jelly,
They tickle their toes and then shake their belly.
With tunes that slide like marbles on floors,
They prank the sun, and it shimmies outdoors.

Oh, the whispers of organs that gulp and sigh,
As they munch on space popcorn, oh so spry!
A chorus of chuckles fills up the air,
As Martians juggle moons without any care.

In this realm of bizarre, all logic's unfurled,
Where gravity's silly, and chaos is swirled.
Let's toast to the laughter, the joy that descends,
From the planets and stars, where the fun never ends!

Verses from the Void of Night

In the silence of the dark, they dance,
Red dust twirls in a cosmic prance.
Alien squirrels give a comic chase,
As they gnaw on chips from Earth's landscape.

Giggles from craters bounce back with glee,
Space bees buzzing in zero gravity.
Martian hats made from old space gear,
Establishing a fashion that's quite the cheer.

Echoed Emotions in Enigmatic Canyons

Down in the canyon, a rubber ball rolls,
Chasing a dust storm that swallows the trolls.
Jovial crickets sing with a quirk,
While spacefarers giggle in a quirky perk.

Wobbling robots learn how to slide,
On dusty slopes, they take a wild ride.
Each tumble and roll brings laughter anew,
Out here in the canyons, fun's overdue!

Nocturnal Notes of the Starry Expanse

Under the stars, the moon takes a bow,
Aliens popping popcorn, the whole crowd's wow.
Silly shadows dance on the surface so bright,
Making the night a whimsical sight.

Laughter echoes as they sip on warm tea,
Complaints from the Earthlings—"This isn't for me!"
But with each giggle beneath the great dome,
They find a strange joy in their cosmic home.

Songs of the Stranded Explorers

Three explorers stranded, they form a band,
Playing with rocks and a rubbery hand.
A toaster as trumpet, a kettle as drum,
Unlikely melodies make their hearts hum.

With each little note, they spin tales galore,
Of the Martian baking that they can't ignore.
Laughing at failures, they sing off-key,
Celebrating the chaos of space, so free!

Dunes of Distant Dreams

In shades of rust, the sandbugs dance,
They twirl and twist, given half a chance.
With tiny hats, they make a parade,
A sight so silly, it can't be delayed.

A cactus sings with a voice quite high,
Echoing secrets to the curious sky.
They giggle as they hoist tiny flags,
While humor blooms like the brightest rags.

Harmonies of the Rocky Veil

Rocky peaks wear wobbly crowns,
With giddy jokes, they wear their gowns.
A slippy slope sings jolly tunes,
Chasing space cows under the moons.

A comet swoops with a crown of cheese,
Winking at astronauts caught in the breeze.
They chuckle and float, with stars in their eyes,
Making silly faces as they rise.

Echoes Beneath the Dusty Skies

Amidst the haze, the echoes shout,
With funny quirks, they dance about.
A tumbleweed in a top hat rolls,
Inviting all to join its strolls.

Beneath a sky of purple bloom,
The whispers giggle of impending doom.
Yet laughter cracks the cosmic seal,
As jokes unfold, surreal yet real.

Ballads of the Blazing Red

In fields of fire where rovers roam,
They strum guitars made of space foam.
A jam session sparks under a star,
While Martian mimes imitate a car.

With laughter bubbling like frothy waves,
They craft wild tales of dashing knaves.
And in the rhythm of outlandish cheer,
Life blooms bizarre in the atmosphere.

Lizard's Lullaby under Red Stars

A lizard sings under crimson skies,
His voice is a croak, oh what a surprise!
He dances with shadows, quite full of glee,
While aliens chuckle, sipping their tea.

His tail sways gently, like a tiny whip,
Each note a giggle, a cosmic trip.
With twinkling stars as his audience fair,
He dreams of planets, and all without care.

Rhapsodic Reflections on Stratosphere

In a rocket ship, I lost my shoe,
Floating up high, oh how I rue!
Saturn's rings took my left foot,
While Martian cats played a wild flute.

They danced in zero-g with a flair so bright,
Their jigs made me laugh, oh what a sight!
With each twirl and spin, I couldn't complain,
Even sans a shoe, it was still quite a gain.

Hymn to the Horizon of Hope

At the horizon, a dragonfly hums,
While purple skies drip in gooey rums.
I waved to a cactus, who waved back slow,
Telling tales of Earth, and how it would glow.

With each little laugh, the red sands did fly,
As martians took selfies, oh me, oh my!
They wore funky hats, with a wink and a grin,
In this horizon full of mischievous whim.

Ballads Beneath Blood Moonlight

Beneath a moon that looks like tomato,
A frog began croaking a tune with bravado.
His friends were a fleet of bizarre space bugs,
They formed a choir, exchanging warm hugs.

They belted out ballads, slightly off-key,
As comets passed by with a chuckle and plea.
With laughter contagious, the night carried on,
Under the blood moon, weirdness was spawned.

Songs of Stellar Desolation

In a land where rocks can talk,
Martians dance, a wobbly walk.
With three left feet and a spindly twirl,
They laugh so loud, watch their hats whirl.

Bouncing cactus, ticklish shade,
They spin around in a funny parade.
Galactic giggles, echoes of cheer,
Who knew space could be so dear?

Searching for joy in a dusty groove,
Their floppy arms break every move.
Cosmos chuckles, stars twinkle bright,
In this lonely place, laughter takes flight.

Oh, the spaceships are always late,
Hurry up, or we'll dance with fate!
Alien tunes from a wobbly hive,
In this void, we truly thrive!

Ballad of the Barren Expanse

In a desert where the boulders grin,
Critters sing with a tickling spin.
Lunar laughter, a cosmic jest,
Who knew boredom could be so blessed?

Dusty dunes of peculiar shape,
With a hop and a skip, let's escape!
Finding joy in a tumble and roll,
Even the craters have a soul.

They toss space seeds in the air,
Watch them sprout with a joyful flare.
Starry shrubs with polka-dot flair,
Every friendship blossoms there.

Oh, listen close, to the echoes sound,
In this barren place, we've truly found.
With giggles floating on cosmic tides,
Together we dance where humor hides.

Melodies of an Alien Landscape

In a land of greenish skies,
Martians wear their space-age ties.
With bubblegum dreams and rockets for shoes,
They giggle with glee, rocking the blues.

Strange fruits giggle from trees that sway,
Calling all creatures to join the play.
Singing of jokes from beyond the sun,
In this surreal world, we all are one.

Purple moons with winking eyes,
Follow the rhythm of comical sighs.
A symphony made of funny mishaps,
Planted in giggles, laid-back claps.

Join the merry band of the spacey crew,
Traveling far with a humorous view.
Laughing through stardust, spinning in bliss,
In an alien land, what could we miss?

Chants of the Cosmic Wind

Whispers of wind in a quirky tone,
Wheeling through space, we're never alone.
Martian kites in a lasting chase,
Floating and flapping through endless space.

They chase the sun, they tickle the stars,
Guided by laughter, no battle scars.
Silly shadows trailing behind,
In this capture-the-fun cosmic grind.

With flutes made of meteors, trumpets of dust,
Creating a tune of cheerful trust.
Strumming the air with jovial glee,
Join in the song, come dance with me.

Oh, the cosmic journey brings quite a thrill,
Riding the waves of the giggling will.
As the universe hums a joyful hymn,
We sway to the rhythm of whimsy's whim.

Lullabies of the Crimson Horizon

In the glow of a red, patchwork sky,
Bouncing space cows leap and fly.
Sounds of laughter fill the air,
While green frogs wear hats with flair.

Dancing rocks in cosmic glee,
Playing hopscotch with a tree.
A comet's tail starts the chase,
As gravity takes a holiday space!

Singing suns with faces bright,
Throwing parties every night.
The sand sings tunes of silly dreams,
While moons twirl in polka beam.

So snuggle close, and take a view,
The universe has laughs for you.
With stars as friends and jokes to share,
Rest easy, cozmic wonder's fair.

Starlit Soliloquy

Underneath a twinkling show,
Aliens paint their faces glow.
Dance on craters, stomp on mugs,
While shooting stars share coffee hugs.

The space-time clock goes tick and tock,
Giggling fools in a timey block.
Gravity's got no hold tonight,
As we kiss the void with sheer delight.

Purple clouds float with a grin,
While spaceships play the banjo's din.
With Martian pizza on the run,
Who knew that space could be this fun?

So if you hear a rocket's song,
Join the chorus, laugh along.
The universe is one big joke,
On this vivid cosmic yoke.

Rhythms of Rust and Dust

Rusty robots tap their feet,
Chasing dust bunnies down the street.
With joints that squeak and laugh so loud,
They gather up a merry crowd.

Underneath the crusty ground,
Silly creatures frolic around.
The sun throws rays like sassy darts,
While goofy spirits steal our hearts.

With a shuffle and a twirl so bright,
They dance away into the night.
The moon grins wide with silver glee,
As cosmic laughter sets them free.

So grab a broom and start to sway,
In rusty rust we find our play.
In every spin and every turning,
The joy of dust is forever burning.

Harmonies Beneath the Canopy

Beneath the shades of purple trees,
Silly creatures sing like bees.
With wobbling voices filled with cheer,
They croak out jokes for all to hear.

Bubbles float in misty air,
As birds sport ties and crazy hair.
They share their worms with giggly frogs,
In a funny world of singing smogs.

The ground hums with a bouncy beat,
As rainbow jelly beans they greet.
With every jump and every shout,
The universe joins in, no doubt!

Under this canopy we sway,
As laughter joins in cosmic play.
So hold your friends and sing along,
In silly vibes, where we belong!

Shadows Singing on Solar Winds

In a dance of cosmic glee,
Aliens giggle under the tree,
With shadows that sway and leap,
They sing secrets that stars keep.

Wind tickles their giddy toes,
Silly hats filled with space hose,
They craft jokes from lunar rays,
While the sun sets in joyful plays.

Each shadow takes a twirling bow,
Declaring how they'd teach a cow,
To sing along in moonlight haze,
With laughter echoing through the days.

Hymns of the Distant Aurora

Under skies of electric blue,
Distant lights chant a tune, so true,
With laughter that sparks in the air,
They jest for the planets, unaware.

Wobbling lights do jig and reel,
Tickling the cosmos with zestful zeal,
In frolicking colors, they boast,
About the space ghosts they like the most.

Electric giggles fill the night,
As they shimmer with pure delight,
Messy hair and polka dot socks,
Dancing around in cosmic flocks.

Stardust Serenades of the Sphinx

A Sphinx in space, how odd it seems,
Telling tales of chocolate dreams,
With stars that drip like honey sweet,
Echoing laughter, a rhythmic beat.

Juggling comets, what a sight!
Gravity rules? Not tonight!
Witty quips from the ancient sage,
In zero-G, they dance on stage.

With a riddle for every snort,
The Sphinx teaches us to cavort,
In stardust aprons, they twirl and spin,
While giggling at the alien kin.

Anthem of the Assembled Planets

As planets gather 'round the sun,
They joke about whose dance is fun,
With wobbling orbits, they grin wide,
Singing tunes of cosmic pride.

Mars winks at Earth, a silly prank,
While Saturn's rings must fill the tank,
They laugh at comets zooming by,
"Hey, keep your tail in check, oh my!"

Venus fumbles with her dress,
At Neptune's jokes, they all confess,
That space is a realm of laughter grand,
In a universe, together they stand.

Lyrical Lament of the Layered Landscape

In landscapes layered with red dust,
A flat rock sits, it truly must.
A shoe's sole stuck, what a sight,
Is it just me, or is this plight?

The winds play games, a swirling breeze,
Whispers of laughter in the trees.
I chuckle loud, the stones agree,
They roll their eyes in harmony.

Giant craters like soup bowls wide,
Invite a dip, a cosmic slide.
But one wrong step, I tumble down,
The dust clouds rise, I wear a crown!

With every bounce, I leap and sway,
Oh, what a fine extraterrestrial day!
Mars, my mate, let's prance about,
In dusty jest, we'll laugh and shout!

Euphony of the Eclipsed Sun

The sun peeked out, then hid in fright,
Behind a cloud—what a quirky sight!
It winked at me with cheerful rays,
I chuckled hard at its hidden plays.

The moon danced in, with a cheeky grin,
Playing hide and seek, oh where to begin?
As shadows stretched across the reddish ground,
My laughter echoed, a joyous sound.

Stars twinkled bright like diamonds on toast,
It's breakfast time, let's all make a toast!
But who would slice the cosmic bread?
Can you believe what the universe bled?

As day fades out and night takes hold,
The whispers of starlight, stories told.
With every twinkle, I hear a pun,
In the theater of skies, we all have fun!

Strophic Stories of Stellar Plains

In stellar plains, where dreams collide,
I stroll along with my furry guide.
A rover's wheel rolls with a squeak,
Joining the chorus of Martian cheek.

With tales of yore from ancient sands,
My imagination's like stretching bands.
Each dune a story, each rock a rhyme,
We laugh with the echoes, it's story time!

Oh, how they tease with jolly jest,
Even the meteors want to rest.
With cosmic giggles that rock and roll,
We dance beneath the starry scroll.

So pass the snacks from cosmic stores,
Let's feast on laughter, and share galore.
In the fun-filled webs of cosmic schemes,
We weave our tales, spun from dreams!

Cantatas of Cosmic Creation

In the cradle of space, a song takes flight,
Notes soar like comets, oh what a sight!
With melodies bright from planets afar,
We jive with the rhythm of each shooting star.

A symphony rises from bases unknown,
Played on instruments made of stone.
Sing, oh space, with a humorous spark,
Echoes of giggles ignite the dark.

As stars collide in a boisterous dance,
They chuckle together in a glittering trance.
What's that twinkling? Oh, just a joke,
The universe giggles, can you hear it poke?

So join the cantatas, sing loud with glee,
In this cosmic concert, you're one with me.
Together we blend, as planets align,
In the funny creation, where all is divine!

Stanzas in the Sands of Time

In the desert, a cactus wears a hat,
It wobbles with pride, oh, imagine that!
A lizard strums tunes on a rock so round,
The mirage dances, not a soul around.

As the sun sets, the shadows begin to play,
A tumbleweed rolls in, seeking its way,
It bumps into rovers, wheels all askew,
They laugh and spin tales, as silly things do.

A sandstorm arrives, like a wild parade,
The cacti all cheer as their hats are displayed,
Instead of gloom, there's laughter and cheer,
Even the sand whispers, "Let's party, my dear!"

So here in the dunes, where the funny winds blow,
The laughter of Martians begins to grow,
From hats to rovers, a curious scene,
In the sands of the time, where all is serene.

The Aria of Abandoned Dreams

A spaceship parked, left to rust and rot,
Once flew endless skies, now it's a plot,
A dreamer's gaze reaches toward the stars,
While little green men munch on candy bars.

They hum a tune of sweet nostalgia's call,
The echoes of laughter within that hull,
Dreams once ambitious now forming a line,
Like Martians with mustaches sipping on brine.

A comet soars past, gives a wink and grin,
"Join us for coffee," it seems to begin,
With sugar and cream, they ponder and plot,
Abandoning dreams, but still finding a spot.

So in this realm, where follies align,
A chorus of humor, life's new design,
Abandoned but bright, with giggles it gleams,
In the aria sung of our silly dreams.

Cadence of the Martian Moons

Two moons twirl in a cosmic ballet,
Each step a giggle, they frolic and sway,
One moon forgot its dance shoes today,
The other just chuckles, "Let's glide, okay?"

They dip and they dive, in a stellar embrace,
While comets throw confetti, what a wild race,
Asteroids bounce, trying to keep in the groove,
Every bounce writes the rhythm; the stars start to move.

Galactic creatures come out for the show,
With green furry hats that steal the moon glow,
They tap in delight to the cadence so bright,
Tickling the void with their dance in the night.

As the night deepens, the waltz will not end,
With laughter and music, the cosmos a friend,
So here's to the moons that dance with such glee,
In a universe swirling wild and carefree.

Requiem for the Lost Descent

With a fizzle and pop, they fell from the sky,
An anchorless rocket that couldn't fly,
Clanged down like a toaster, what a loud scene,
The Martians all laughed, "Was that brave or mean?"

They gathered around, with snacks in their hands,
Analyzing landing mishaps in bands,
Popsicle sticks were the launch pads of choice,
Constructing new ships with giggles and noise.

An alien pondered, "What's the point of this?"
While nibbling on chips and a marshmallow kiss,
Then came an idea, absurd but so sweet,
"Let's host a party, with dance and a treat!"

And so, in the dust, the lost descent turned,
Into a festival, where friendships confirmed,
In laughter they soared, through the cosmos they pranced,
In a requiem joyous, where no one was chanced.

Starlit Tales from the Void

In a galaxy far, squirrels fly,
Chasing cheese with a twinkle in their eye.
Asteroids dance, they bust a groove,
While green ants groove in a zero-gravity move.

Comets whiz past, like rockets on fire,
Space cats sing to their heart's desire.
With laughter echoing through the cosmic night,
Even black holes giggle, what a funny sight!

Stars wear hats made of space debris,
Sending signals out, saying, "Come see me!"
Moon pies float on stardust streams,
Who knew cosmic snacks could fulfill our dreams?

So grab your friends, let's leap and bound,
In the vacuum, laughter will resound.
Let's tell these tales from beyond the light,
In this void, every moment feels just right.

Melodies Under the Martian Moon

Beneath the glow of a ruby sky,
Space frogs croak and wonders fly.
They strum their banjos made of ice,
With each pluck, the stars add spice.

Dishwasher aliens join the tune,
Spinning plates under the Martian moon.
Clumsy robots kick up the dust,
Their two-left-feet just bust my trust.

Plastic flutes play a funky beat,
As dancing craters party on their feet.
Small creatures wearing snorkels and hats,
Break out the chips, let's rock the mats!

As we groove under this rusty light,
The melodies, oh what a delight!
Each note brings us to crazy heights,
Making memories on these cosmic nights.

Verses of a Forgotten World

In dusty dreams where no one roams,
The chairs play chess and build their homes.
Curtains flap like wings on a spree,
While the lost socks gossip: "What about me?"

Quiet plants plot an E.T. tease,
While rocks complain of past due fees.
Fairy lights buzz on futuristic strings,
They relay secrets of Martian kings.

Old toys laugh in the cosmic air,
Telling tales of joy, with a hint of flair.
Forgotten worlds have much to say,
If you listen close, they'll brighten your day.

So come along, let's dance in the dust,
Embrace the funny, it's a cosmic must.
In verses penned on a crumpled page,
These forgotten worlds share joy with sage.

Lyric of the Rusted Horizon

On this rusty plane where robots dream,
They sip on oil and plot their scheme.
Muffin tops float 'round on cosmic breeze,
As comets giggle and wobbly trees.

Vintage tunes from old radios moan,
As lonesome meteors throw a stone.
Space mice skitter, catch a tune,
Dancing under the swoon of the moon.

Gears clank, and sparks begin to fly,
Beneath a blanket of an electric sky.
With rusty hearts, we sing our song,
In this rhythm where we all belong.

So let's revel in this quirky sight,
Under the horizon, gleaming bright.
With laughter ringing, we'll share the fun,
Each lyric a spark 'til the day is done.

The Song of the Sundered Sky

In a land where green is rare,
Aliens dance without a care.
They juggle rocks like shiny toys,
And laugh out loud with thrilling joys.

Balloons float high, in colors bright,
A parade of stars comes out at night.
With tinfoil hats and cosmic tunes,
They croon to cats and barking moons.

Fluffy clouds made of cotton cheer,
As giggles echo far and near.
Martian lakes with lemonade tease,
Come sip with us, if you please!

So here's to skies forever blue,
Where whims and wonders come anew.
In this odd place, absurd and grand,
The universe is just a band!

Melodies of Martian Mysteries

Bouncing beetles hum a tune,
While little critters dance at noon.
With ukuleles made of mud,
They strum a song, a joyful thud.

A purple cactus starts to sway,
As silly shadows join the play.
They twist and turn in perfect sync,
While sipping on a drink of pink.

Clouds of jelly drift on by,
As candy comets paint the sky.
A polka here, a waltz or two,
Martian music's made for you!

With giggling stars around the bend,
The laughter of the cosmos blends.
A symphony of songs and glee,
Join in the fun, come dance with me!

Soliloquies in Silent Sands

In deserts vast where silence reigns,
A wise old rock complains in chains.
It tells tall tales of ancient days,
Where laughter rang in sunny rays.

Sand dunes roll like playful waves,
With secrets that the lost wind saves.
A tumbleweed with jokes to share,
It tickles up the evening air.

Eclipsed by sun's bright, burning glow,
The shadows waltz, as all winds blow.
A symphony of grains that chime,
Crafting laughter, one grain at a time.

So laugh aloud at tales of sand,
With every grain, a joke is planned.
In quiet corners, fun resides,
In every whisper, joy abides!

The Chorus of Cosmic Whispers

In a galaxy far, far away,
Whispers giggle, dance, and play.
Stars exchange their flirty winks,
While comets scribble silly links.

Asteroids that wear bright hats,
Join choirs full of bouncing chats.
Singing rockets zoom with grace,
As laughter lights up every space.

Planets spin, a dizzy dance,
Galactic jesters take a chance.
With every twirl, a chuckle flows,
In cosmic realms where humor glows.

So tune your ears to laughter's grace,
Space is a grand, funny place.
With whispers that delight the night,
The universe is pure delight!

Verses from the Valley of Valles Marineris

In the valley deep, where shadows tease,
A roving rover sings to the Martian breeze.
With wheels that squeak and lights that blink,
It hums a tune, though it's not in sync.

Dusty dunes dance like they're on a spree,
As rocks laugh softly at the sight they see.
Little green men with a penchant for pranks,
Join in the chorus, giving jolly thanks.

Shadows grow long as the sun starts to dip,
Martian critters gather for a cosmic trip.
They twirl and they whirl, in a merry parade,
While UFOs hover, unperturbed and unafraid.

So raise up your glass to the odd and the strange,
In the valley of wonder, where nothing can change.
For in every giggle, and in every cheer,
There's joy in the cosmos, and laughter is near.

Twilight Tunes of Terra Cotta

Beneath the sky, in hues of clay,
The twilight sings, as night greets day.
With crickets chirping a not-so-cool rhyme,
And Martian mice dancing to the beat of the time.

There's a party of rocks, with hats made of dust,
They groove and they move, it's a cosmic must.
In the shadowy glow, a comet whizzes by,
And all the stars twinkle, in the velvet sky.

Laughter erupts with a comical shout,
As a space squirrel struts, full of cosmic clout.
He juggles the stars, or so it would seem,
While Martian owls hoot—it's all a big dream.

So grab a moon pie, and take a big bite,
Join the twirling fun in the pale moonlight.
In Terra Cotta's glow, let your heart take flight,
For silly tunes echo, soft and bright!

Dirges of Distant Echoes

In the canyons wide, where silence reigns,
Echoes of laughter still rattle the chains.
A ghost from the past runs in circles for fun,
Chasing comets and dreams, oh what a run!

Down canyons and hills, they glide with a cheer,
Each note from the void gently floats to your ear.
A melancholy tune with a twist of delight,
As the echoes grow richer in the pale moonlight.

Singing to stars that are way out of view,
With voices like fizz, and a chorus of goo.
Distant figures dance, in shadows they play,
Twirling and swirling, till the end of the day.

So listen intently to the faraway sound,
Let the echoes of laughter in the cosmos abound.
For in every dirge, a giggle does hide,
In the echoes of space, let joy be your guide.

The Symphony of Solitude

In solitude's embrace, a whimsical tune,
A lone martian hums, swaying under the moon.
With rocks as his friends, and craters for cheer,
He spins in delight, spreading joy far and near.

With each little note, a comet takes flight,
Through the silence so loud, and the cosmic night.
He bows to the stars, gives a wink to the sun,
Swaying through stardust, just having some fun.

His symphony's quirky, with beats so absurd,
A soundtrack of giggles, from each passing bird.
With trumpets of wind, and guitars made of light,
This solo so merry brings the dark to bright.

So join in the song, let your spirit be free,
In the solitude grand, sing along with glee.
For in every note, there's a spark and a jest,
In the symphony of space, we are truly blessed.

Reverberations of the Remote Reality

In the silence of red dust,
A marching band of ants we trust.
They play their tunes with serious flair,
While I float above without a care.

The sun wears sunglasses, oh so bright,
As shadows dance in quirky flight.
Rovers spin like merry-go-rounds,
While laughter echoes off the mounds.

With rocks that sing a fiddler's tune,
And sunsets painted by a loon.
I sway and giggle under stars,
In a world where laughter heals the scars.

The Tune of Twilit Trails

A cactus whispers jokes at night,
While glowing orbs take wing in flight.
They twirl around on silent wings,
As moonbeams laugh with silver strings.

Dancing dust with giggle fits,
And red clouds hurling playful hits.
Jelly craters bounce to the beat,
As Martian critters tap their feet.

With twinkling stars in generous cheer,
Each chuckle echoes, drawing near.
On trails of twilight, wander we,
In this whimsical harmony.

Lyrical Legends of Lost Valleys

In valleys where the giggles roam,
Whimsical creatures find a home.
They strum on rocks with glee and grace,
As legends smile in endless space.

Each hill holds tales of grand delight,
Where shadows play hide and seek at night.
Laughter lingers like the breeze,
Invisible tickles in the trees.

With stories etched in rusty red,
Of talking boulders and much misled.
I tuck in dreams of charming bands,
Performing joy with playful hands.

The Echoing Silence of Distant Dreams

In the silence, echoes cheer and jest,
While stars throw parties, never rest.
A comet jokes, with a cheeky wink,
As galaxies pause to share a drink.

Nighttime cuddles with whispers low,
While playful meteors put on a show.
They streak across with laughter's burst,
In cosmic jest they quench their thirst.

The dreams that drift on cosmic streams,
Are filled with laughter, bursting seams.
As shadowy figures sway and play,
In a universe, bright and gay.

Celestial Serenade

Under the stars, a green bug dances,
With eight tiny legs, it takes its chances.
Eating the dust of cosmic delight,
It twirls and it sways, oh what a sight!

A floating rock joins in on the fun,
Singing off-key by the blazing sun.
The moon winks slyly, as asteroids race,
In this wacky world, we find our place.

Jupiter laughs, while Saturn spins rings,
Even the comets wear glittering bling.
A chorus of laughter fills the night air,
In this cosmic party, there's joy everywhere!

With aliens prancing, it's quite the show,
A merry parade in a wide cosmic glow.
We dance on the red, with joy and with zeal,
Oh, how strange it is, but what a great deal!

Red Planet Reveries

A quirky rover rolled down the street,
With wheels made of cheese, oh what a treat!
It stopped for a drink at a Martian bar,
Where sandstorms meet lattes, oh my, how bizarre!

The sunsets are purple, the clouds are green,
No one knows quite what the sunsets mean.
But all the inhabitants giggle with glee,
As they toast to the moon with warm Martian tea.

One creature wore socks with polka dots bright,
It danced through the caves in sheer delight.
Gravity's low, and the jumps are so high,
A game of hopscotch, reaching for the sky!

As rockets zoom past with a splash and a boom,
We chuckle together in our crimson room.
Serenading the stars, oh what a delight,
Life on this red globe is funny and bright!

Songs from the Crimson Expanse

In the valleys of red where the dust bunnies play,
Martians giggle and joke through the whole day.
With rubbery limbs and eyes that can blink,
They share their wild tales while sipping on pink.

A cactus with arms offers free hugs,
While spinning around, shocking all the bugs.
They sing ancient tunes with a twist of the fates,
Bouncing and bouncing, oh isn't it great?

The valleys vibrate with laughter and cheer,
Even the rocks seem to chuckle near.
Stargazing antics in a flash of a night,
Under the colorful skies, all feels just right!

As comets tail us with permissions to play,
We dance on the sand till the break of day.
Living like this, oh what a fun fest,
In the crimson expanse, we are truly blessed!

Whispers of the Cosmic Wind

A breeze carried whispers from across the stars,
Tickling the antennas of our singing bizarre.
A fish in the sky, a bird in the sea,
The worlds flipped and twirled, oh how could it be?

With giggles and chuckles, the cosmos spry,
A starfish sings songs while floating on by.
Each planet's a stage, with life at center,
Jokes flying high like a comet's splendor!

Celestial jesters parade through the space,
They tumble and turn with an elegant grace.
Rockets and rockets, what a noisy ballet,
Each one more wacky than yesterday's play!

The laughter erupts from globes round and wide,
With cosmic confetti, we float in the tide.
In the arms of the wind, whimsy takes flight,
These whispers of joy keep us warm in the night!

Sagas Written in Cosmic Sand

In the dark where grains do twirl,
A worm in a space suit starts to swirl.
He lost his hat while dancing 'round,
Pretending to be the king of sound.

His friends all laughed and cheered with glee,
As he juggled chips from a strange old tree.
They held a banquet with moonlight stew,
While the stars all giggled—how silly, too!

The comet's tail lit up the sky,
As aliens waved and asked him why.
He shrugged and danced with twinkling grace,
In this odd, enchanting, starry place.

With space tacos and a galactic band,
Together they made their cosmic stand.
A tale of laughter, cheers, and fun,
Written in sand 'neath the alien sun.

Chants of the Starry Wilderness

In the wilds where starlight flows,
A critter sings with a honk and a nose.
His dancing feet kick up the dust,
While smart-aleck moons bestow their trust.

Around the rocks, they all would hop,
Making melodies that never stop.
The galaxies joined with a ripple of sound,
As laughter echoed and joy was found.

With jellybeans raining from above,
Each shot a wish, each drip a love.
The critter smiled with a twinkle and spin,
Singing harmonies where dreams begin.

In the wilderness of cosmic bliss,
Every star shared a cheeky kiss.
Together they danced till the end of night,
In the hilarious glow of ethereal light.

Echoing Through the Ether

In the ether where oddities meet,
A dragon on roller skates takes a seat.
He twirls and spins, but oops! He falls,
Bouncing back up with laughter calls.

The nebula chuckled, the black hole swayed,
As planets chimed in, their tones conveyed.
The cosmic DJ played a tune so sweet,
Everyone grooved to the funky beat.

With glowing sprinkles and flying pies,
Each mishap brought whimsical surprise.
A hula-hoop comet sparked in delight,
While squirrels on broomsticks soared out of sight.

And in this realm of quirk and cheer,
Friendships blossomed, year after year.
Echoing laughter, a celestial ring,
In the spry atmosphere, joy takes wing.

Poems of the Solar Odyssey

In a rocket made of cheese and dreams,
They traveled far on moonlit beams.
With party hats and jelly roll,
Every explorer had a dancing soul.

They laughed at moons bouncing like balls,
At Saturn's rings—the best of stalls.
A picnic on Mars, with sandwiches that dance,
Made the journey feel like a galactic romance.

Shooting stars served us fizzy drinks,
While aliens painted cosmic pinks.
Each verse of adventure, a funny twist,
As they charted the sky, who could resist?

With laughter echoing from planet to star,
They wrote their tales, no matter how bizarre.
In this solar bound saga of laughter and cheer,
The odyssey continued, year after year.

Lullabies from an Alien Shore

Beneath a sky of purple hues,
The creatures dance in wild shoes.
With winks and grins, they sing away,
As stars join in the cosmic play.

They sway upon the glimmering sand,
With laughter stretching, hand in hand.
A tune so sweet, it tickles the mind,
While space-time bends and unwinds.

Glowbugs flash like disco lights,
As aliens flaunt their funny sights.
They play hide and seek with a comet's tail,
Chasing dreams like a playful gale.

In gentle waves, the lullabies flow,
Where every sound is a ticklish blow.
So sleep, dear stars, in this gleeful land,
Where joy and wonder ever stand.

Notes of Nebula Nights

Under a blanket of shimmering stars,
A flock of pink llamas plays guitars.
They strum their strings, with furry flair,
As alien critters dance in the air.

A tuba blares with a honk and a toot,
While moon mice groove in their silly suits.
Every note a giggle, every chord a cheer,
The cosmos joins in, oh dear, oh dear!

Jupiter winks, with a gassy grin,
And Saturn spins in a merry spin.
The symphony glows like a disco ball,
As laughter echoes in the celestial hall.

So let the night with melody ring,
With snickers and jokes and little things.
In nebula nights, let the silliness flow,
Trust the universe to steal the show!

Rhapsody of the Red Desert

In the red dunes, where the sun does smile,
Sandworms twist in a goofy style.
They wiggle and jiggle, what a bizarre show,
As aliens munch on some galactic dough.

With cactus hats and mismatched socks,
They gather round to tell silly knocks.
Each story spins in a joyful whirl,
As the desert glows with an alien twirl.

Dancing shadows do the cactus cha-cha,
While crazy crickets chirp "Olé!" with bravado.
A comet zips past with a cheeky wink,
As they laugh and tumble, making us think.

Oh, in this rhapsody, joy takes flight,
As the sun dips low, wrapping up the night.
Red desert tales spun with delight,
Where humor bursts with cosmic light.

Odes of Astral Winds

On cosmic breezes, the laughter flows,
As fluffy clouds don funny clothes.
With ticklish winds that swirl and spin,
The stars are merry, let the fun begin!

Planets play tag, racing through space,
While comets giggle, swirling with grace.
From here to there, the breezes carry,
The tales of aliens, quirky and merry.

Galaxies twirl in a dizzying dance,
While the black holes chuckle at their chance.
Through the silence, a chuckle breaks,
As stardust trails turn into pranks.

So let the odes of astral winds weave,
With every whisper, there's room to believe.
In a universe swirling with playful love,
Funny moments lie just above.

Ballads at Dusk on Dione

In the twilight glow, aliens dance,
With tentacles waving, they take a chance.
Frogs in spacesuits croak a tune,
While turtles play chess under a goofy moon.

Martians mime the waltz with glee,
Chasing after floating cups of tea.
A picnic under bubbles, sweet and grand,
As pink skittles rain from a candy land.

The stars laugh loudly in the purple sky,
A disco ball spins, oh my, oh my!
Crackers pop and rockets zoom,
While gummy bears rise, looking for a room.

Everyone giggles, what a sight!
In the funkiest place, all feels right.
Dione shines with laughter bright,
As bubbly beings twirl into the night.

Nocturnes of New Horizons

On a comet's tail, a penguin slides,
With ice cream cones, it joyfully rides.
They sing silly songs, oh what a show,
While craters turn red from the laughter flow.

Planets spin with a goofy grace,
Aliens playing hopscotch in outer space.
Jokers throw pies—what a fantastic scene,
As Saturn's rings dance to the jester's gleam.

Shooting stars wink, and black holes yawn,
In a merry parade, they keep on going on.
Bigfoot juggles moons, it's quite the trend,
And space-time bends; we never want it to end.

With rubber bands, they launch and fly,
Creating constellations of each silly guy.
At the edge of the universe, joy does ignite,
As giggles echo through the endless night.

Hymns from the Heavens Above

Over the clouds, a chicken floats,
In a rocket ship, with songs it gloats.
Singing to stars, it twirls and spins,
While the cosmos chuckles, where fun begins.

Giraffes in tutus prance on Mars,
Waving at astronauts and their flying cars.
Squirrels juggle asteroids in a game,
Cheering loudly as they shout their names.

Neptune's teacups laugh and cheer,
For fanciful tea parties held each year.
Bubbles rise high, colors burst,
As comet tails twinkle and brightly thirst.

With a wink from the moon and a wink from the sun,
The universe dances, it's all just fun.
Each hymn a riff of laughter and cheer,
In the galaxy's heart, joy's always near.

Echoes of an Untamed Dream

In a playground built of asteroid charms,
Kids with antennas spread comic arms.
Hopscotch on Moonbeams, they jump and play,
While laughter rings out in an interstellar ballet.

A bear in a tutu sings to his cat,
In a rocket ship wearing a party hat.
They dance 'round stars that blink and flip,
Launching joy from a happy quip.

Space whales hum tunes that tickle the soul,
As jellybeans orbit and swirl with control.
The galaxy giggles, oh what a sight,
As colors twirl in the dazzling light.

When aliens whisper secrets to trees,
Understanding life amongst the galaxies.
A melody floats, like candy it streams,
In this whimsical realm of untamed dreams.

Songs of the Fading Sun

When the sun sits low, a tasty treat,
An alien chef keeps time with his feet.
He stirs cosmic stew, a sight quite absurd,
With laughter and joy that's utterly blurred.

As shadows grow long, they dance on the dunes,
Singing sweet songs to the clanging tunes.
A robot choir croaks, in off-key delight,
While space critters jive, under blueberry light.

Stars blink their eyes, they giggle anew,
Yet one little star forgot what to do.
He twirled on his axis, then fell on his face,
Creating a cosmic, most comical, space.

So let's grab a drink, from a fizzy red can,
And toast to the dusk, with a goofy grin plan.
For laughter up here is the best kind of fun,
As we sing our bright songs, till the day is all done.

Chimes of Celestial Winds

The wind whistles tunes, like a toddler with glee,
While cactus-ettes shimmy, oh so merrily!
A spaceship nearby, blossoms puffs of green,
It's a wacky parade, that's just too obscene.

Galactic hiccups echo through space,
As Martians juggle moons, with a clumsy grace.
Their hats made of stardust, their shoes made of cheese,
A giggle erupts, carried far on the breeze.

With telescopes peeking, oh what do they find?
A squabble of aliens, of the funniest kind!
They argue for hours over bubblegum size,
While the cosmos above just rolls its bright eyes.

So dance with the planets, twirl with the sun,
Embrace all the quirks, 'cause we're all here for fun!
In the vastness of space, joy's the magical thread,
Binding us tightly, as we laugh 'till we're red.

Ballads of the Martian Sands

In the dusty red hills, laughter can bloom,
As critters in helmets put on quite a show.
They leap and they bounce, with musical glee,
While spinning in circles, oh how do they flow!

A zany old rover rides down on a slide,
Splashing in puddles of cosmic confusion.
While satellites giggle, and tumble like toys,
Creating a ruckus, with no real conclusion.

The ground shakes with joy, as they stomp all around,
Making music with footsteps on soft alien ground.
Serenading the stars, in tunes wildly spun,
With antics so silly, they forgot all the fun!

So gather your laughter, and spread it like sand,
Blend joy with each heartbeat, in this wacky land.
'Cause who wouldn't join in, this chaos so grand,
When even the universe is part of the band?

Lyrical Echoes From Afar

From peaks of high craters, where giggles do flow,
A chorus of aliens sing songs of their woe.
Yet woe becomes joy, as their tales are retold,
With a twist of bright humor, and a sprinkle of gold.

"Hey look at my shoes!" cries a slug with a grin,
"I found them on Earth, they don't fit, but I win!"
The stars twinkle down, sprinkling light on their jest,
As wisdom they share, in a laughter-filled quest.

With comets as dancers, they swirl through the night,
While planets join hands in the soft starlit light.
It's a show never seen, a spectacle bright,
With chuckles and cheer, that takes flight in the night.

So sing with abandon, let your spirits all soar,
For humor's the melody that we can't ignore.
In echoes from afar, where the wide cosmos plays,
We'll laugh through the ages, in the silliest ways.

Melodic Ghosts of Gorgon

In the desert of dust, they dance and creep,
With a wink of their eyes, they never sleep.
Playing hopscotch with rocks, what a sight,
They sing to the stars in the pale moonlight.

Whispers of laughter in the canyon's bend,
A chorus of chuckles that never end.
In the craters they frolic, in joy they twirl,
As the red planet spins, they give it a swirl.

With comets for hats and asteroids for shoes,
They party on Mars, spreading cosmic blues.
Jiving with meteors that glide and zoom,
Creating a rhythm that lights up the gloom.

Oh, those ghosts in the dust, so lively and spry,
Phantom entertainers who dance through the sky.
Their antics are silly, their humor so bright,
As they tease us with laughter, a pleasing delight.

Vagabond Verses on Valles

Down in the valleys where shadows play,
The vagabonds hum through night and day.
With a twist of their tails and a laugh so grand,
They strut through the dunes, a quirky band.

They trade silly riddles with the rocks and the breeze,
Spinning tall tales that bring us to knees.
In the whispers of wind, their giggles resound,
As they bounce off the walls with frolic abound.

Chasing after echoes of their own carefree song,
They dance with the dust, where all creatures belong.
Their whimsy is woven in every small breeze,
Creating a joy that is sure to please.

With a wink and a grin, they tumble and roll,
In the valleys of color, they're always on a stroll.
So raise up your glass to these merry fools,
For in the land of laughter, they make the rules.

Odes to the Orbiting Stars

Orbiting brightly, they spin with flair,
Twinkling like jesters, up in the air.
They whisper sweet secrets to the curious night,
Sending giggles through galaxies, what a delight!

One star trips over another, a luminescent spill,
While others catch comets just for the thrill.
They ride on the tails of the solar winds' race,
In this cosmic cabaret, they find their place.

Chasing the shadows of planets so bold,
Their luminary laughter's a sight to behold.
In this dance of the heavens, so merry and wise,
They captivate all with their sparkling surprise.

An ode to these stars, dancing carefree in line,
A gala of giggles, a festival divine.
With every twinkle, they spread joy afar,
Laughing together, each one a bright star.

Serenades in the Shadow of Olympus

In the shadow of mountains where Martians sing,
Laughter erupts, oh what joy they bring!
Bubble up tunes that echo so wide,
As they dance with the shadows, full of pride.

Atop Olympus, they gather in glee,
Crafting sweet serenades, oh so carefree.
With harmonies soft as a comet's tail glow,
They strum on their lyres made from space snow.

Dressed in bright colors like flowers in bloom,
They spin tales that banish all traces of gloom.
Their voices like gold add spice to the air,
These merry performers with sparkles to share.

Join the sweet festivity, feel the delight,
As they serenade under the starry night.
With a wink and a puff of a magical tune,
They fill the vast cosmos, a joyous festoon.

Tunes from the Hushed Abyss

In a corner of space, where the dust bunnies play,
The aliens dance in a waltz made of clay.
With their three wiggly legs and a hum like a bee,
They sing silly songs, just for you and me.

Craters and canyons, a marvelous sight,
A cosmic parade of giggles at night.
They juggle the stars, toss the asteroids high,
While laughing at Earth as their rockets fly by.

Bouncing on moons, with their heads in the clouds,
Throw in some robots, and we'll gather crowds.
With joy in their circuits and laughter in gears,
These interstellar clowns have no fears.

So tune in your ears to the silence so loud,
Where quirky little creatures make us all proud.
Join the cosmic circus, take a space ride,
In the tunes from the hush, let's all laugh and glide.

Celestial Serenades

Under the stars, where the quirks intertwine,
The quasar quartets play Sonatas divine.
With flutes made of stardust and drums of pure light,
They serenade planets on a whimsical night.

Comets are dancers, tails trailing bright,
They spin and they twirl, such a marvelous sight.
While the moons hum a tune in a jazzy refrain,
Even silence will chuckle, forgetting its pain.

Shooting stars pop like popcorn in flight,
As the universe giggles, a side-splitting sight.
With each cosmic note, let our worries all fade,
In a symphony where shadows are played.

So gather around as the orbits align,
In a celestial ball where worlds intertwine.
With laughter and joy, let's take to the sky,
And dance in the rhythms where dreams never die.

Echoes of a Forgotten World

On a planet far off, where the cactus trees sing,
Echoes of laughter in a cosmic swing.
With forgotten old tales of space-time so vast,
Wormholes and giggles from the colorful past.

Dust devils whirl with a comedic charm,
Sowing smiles and comfort, like a cozy warm balm.
They tickle the surface of the Mars reddish spree,
Where rocks tell the truth over cups of green tea.

With castles made of clouds drifting lazily by,
And pools with confetti that bubble and sigh.
Invisible creatures throw parties at dawn,
With jazz hands and snacks made of stardust and yarn.

So let's toast to the echoes, delightful and bright,
Of a world long forgotten, yet dancing with light.
In laughter and wonder, we'll bask in the glow,
As we revel in stories of merriment flow.

Whispers on the Red Soil

On the red dusty plains, where the jokers reside,
Whispers of nonsense in the Martian tide.
With hats made of craters and smiles so wide,
They chuckle at comets who nervously glide.

Roses of rust bloom, with petals of fun,
Each beam of sunlight is a laugh on the run.
Aliens play hide and seek with the stars,
Hiding behind rocks, throwing candy from cars.

As twinkling toast parties take front stage now,
With the moon as their waiter, it takes a big bow.
And when the sun sets, they toast with their chips,
To the joy of the cosmos, with laughter that rips.

So join in the whisper, let giggles unfold,
On this red rocky planet, where stories are bold.
In the theater of space, take your seat and unwind,
As the whispers keep spinning, leaving worries behind.

The Ballad of the Beloved Barrens

In the dust of red, we dance and spin,
With a twirl of dust, let the fun begin.
Aliens peek with their multiple eyes,
Laughing at us with their cosmic sighs.

Sandstorms swirl like a wild old cat,
Chasing our hats; oh where are they at?
We tumble and roll in the barren expanse,
While the craters below do a silly old dance.

Rovers on scooters glide past with glee,
Waving their flags like they're carefree.
They sing little songs of their robotic pride,
As we join in with laughter, swinging wide.

Under the stars, we set up our camp,
Roasting red marshmallows like an off-world champ.
With comets as guests, we revel all night,
In the beloved barrens, oh what a sight!

Harmonies in Hazy Atmospheres

Under skies of fog, we croon and jest,
With floating guitars and a saxophone zest.
Martians tap dance with their eight little toes,
To the rhythm of laughter that everyone knows.

Hazy horizons shimmer with cheer,
As we serenade friends who float near.
With bubble machines puffing bright blue,
We create a spectacle, a cosmic review.

Our voices carry on the soft, still air,
Echoing giggles, no worries or care.
We sing of the moons and the stars high above,
In harmonies sweet, wrapped in friendship and love.

With lasers that twinkle and sprites in the dark,
Our absurdity trails like a comet's bright spark.
In these hazy atmospheres, we find our own glee,
A chorus of hilarity, come join us and see!

Echoes of an Otherworldly Heart

In the valleys of echoes, our voices collide,
With a chorus of quirks that we cannot hide.
Each hiccup and giggle reverberates bright,
A symphony strange, but a pure delight.

Alien critters join in our song,
With their honks and their beeps, nothing feels wrong.
They twirl in the air like they've lost their way,
While we cheer them on with a merry ballet.

Under the moons, we skip and we play,
In otherworldly vibes, we shall sway.
With loony chants of green cheese and rock,
We create a spectacle that will surely shock.

So here in this land, with laughter we'll chart,
The echoes of joy from an otherworldly heart.
Where absurdity reigns and all is carefree,
We'll sing to the stars, come dance along with me!

Refrains of the Rusty Terrain

In rusty red hills, we frolic and play,
Rolling down slopes in a zany ballet.
Our knees are now stained with Martian clay,
Laughing so much, we could brighten the day.

With squelchy old boots, we stomp through the muck,
In this strange little world, we've thrown out the luck.
Gravity swings like a jester on strings,
As we leap and we twirl, oh what joy it brings!

The sky's filled with sparkles, the ground with delight,
We spin 'round the craters till the stars are in sight.
Each tumble and fall is a badge of our cheer,
In the rusty terrain, we've nothing to fear.

So gather your friends, let the silliness flow,
In this quirky terrain, laughter's our show.
As the sun sets low, we'll cherish the fun,
In refrains of joy, we'll all be as one!

The Rhythm of Cosmic Silence

In the stillness of space, I dance with glee,
A cosmic waltz with a squishy pea.
The stars are laughing, what a sight to see,
They jiggle and wobble, just like me!

My spaceship squeaks, it sounds a bit crude,
But it plays a tune that's simply a hoot!
A galaxy band with a funky mood,
Where asteroids twirl in an interstellar suit.

I twirl past Mars with a goofy grin,
Waving to robots who join in the spin.
We hula with comets, let the fun begin,
In the rhythm of silence, we all fit right in!

Down in the craters, a party awaits,
With cosmic confetti and celestial plates.
We feast on stardust and dance till it's late,
In a giggle-filled space, we celebrate fate!

Sonnet of the Scarlet Rocks

Oh, scarlet rocks, how you tease my eyes,
Like giant cherries under sapphire skies.
I trip over pebbles, but still I rise,
In a comedy show of Martian surprise!

The dust storms howl with a cheeky wink,
They tickle my toes as I step to the brink.
I ponder their secrets, with a wink and a blink,
Creating wild stories that make me think.

I thought I met aliens, a quirky bunch,
They offered me cookies and a fizzy punch.
But I ran when I noticed they wanted to munch,
On my favorite snacks; no way, that's a crunch!

So here I stand, on these rust-red plains,
With laughter echoing in Martian domains.
The rocks keep giggling; I shout with refrains,
In the land of the funny, where joy never wanes!

Aria of the Cosmic Dunes

Oh, cosmic dunes, like waves of candy,
I surf on your surfaces, feeling quite dandy.
The grains giggle softly, ever so handy,
In a sugary dream where life is all sandy.

I met a sand monster; he wore a big hat,
With a smile so wide, and he liked to chat.
We swapped silly jokes, he laughed like a brat,
But his voice was a whisper, "Watch out for that!"

For hiding below are the ticklish boulders,
Who chuckle and rumble as they grow older.
They trip up my feet, making me colder,
In this snow-like landscape; oh, what a shoulder!

So I'll dance with the dunes, and laugh with the breeze,
As the sun sets low, giving me a tease.
Underneath it all, I say with such ease,
In the aria of fun, may I never please!

Chronicles Under the Martian Sky

Beneath the bold sky, a tale spins around,
Of chuckling aliens who dance on the ground.
They juggle the stars and make silly sounds,
In the chronicles where pure laughter's found.

With glowing green faces, they tell me of fun,
How they race with the comets, each whimsical run.
I fetch a few tacos, avoiding the sun,
And join in the mischief, giggling overdone!

With each twinkling star, they teach me to laugh,
We sketch cosmic doodles that feel like a gaffe.
In this interstellar huddle, I'm a creative staff,
Painting Martian mischief, we're always on draft!

So here's to the joy of the Martian night,
With chuckles and giggles and pure delight.
In this cosmic corner, everything feels right,
In chronicles woven, we dance with insight!

Choral Echoes in the Starlit Night

Beneath the bright, twinkling stars,
A tune is hummed, oh so bizarre.
Alien creatures dance with glee,
Flapping their wings, like an old parakeet.

With cosmic giggles they cover the ground,
Singing along to the echoing sound.
The moon cracks jokes, oh what a sight,
As laughter spills into the night.

They stomp on the Mars dust, making a mess,
Wobbling around in their funny dress.
One drops a snack, oh what a blunder,
A feast for the ants, they dance and wonder.

So if you hear a chorus take flight,
Know it's just aliens, laughing with delight.
In the starlit night, joy takes a wing,
Echoes of giggles are what they sing.

Poetry of the Parched Wind

The wind whispers tales of goofy events,
Of Martian folks with peculiar scents.
They scribble their poems in bright orange dust,
Claiming it's art—well, we must adjust!

With hula-hoops spun from rusty old rods,
They laugh at the Earthlings as if they're gods.
A tumble, a trip in their awkward grace,
The wind just chuckles, like it's a race!

Somersaults in space, what a sight to behold,
They spin like tops, yet never grow old.
With dry humor, they dance in the sun,
Chasing shadows and having some fun.

Oh, the tales the dry air would tell,
Of windy capers that cast a spell.
In a world so red, laughter does thrive,
A quirk in the breeze keeps them alive.

Verses on the Verge of No Return

On a rock in the void, they ponder and sway,
In search of a laugh to brighten the day.
Juggling red pebbles, they aim for the stars,
What a sight it is—those silly Martian bazars!

With a wink and a nod, they express their delight,
Silly alien dances in the pale moonlight.
Two-stepping round, not a worry or care,
Tripping on craters with laughter to share.

Their humor is vast, much like their plains,
Bouncing ideas like wacky refrains.
Leaping past logic, they find their own way,
To joke about life in their zany ballet.

But out in space, as they giggle and twirl,
They hover on edges that twist and unfurl!
What's this? A chorus? They clamor and cheer—
In the world of the absurd, they conquer their fear.

Serenades Over the Silent Abyss

In the quiet of space, they raise their voice,
Strumming guitars, making noise by choice.
With creatures that dance, they serenade night,
The silent abyss is filled with delight.

They croon to the stars, oh how they shine,
With funky little steps, they claim it's divine.
No worries about time, they play with a grin,
Singing to worlds where the wild nonsense begins.

Bubbles of laughter float up in the air,
While juggling strange fruits without a care.
With daft little moves, they skip on the brink,
The abyss below, yet they still get a wink!

So raise up your glasses, or whatever you pour,
Join the jubilant party, let's laugh some more!
In the vast, empty dark, joy dances and spins,
Echoes of fun where their adventure begins.

Rhapsody in Red and Gold

In a land where dust bunnies dance,
Aliens giggle in their bright pants.
Jupiter's rings are made of cheese,
And Martians tease the cosmic breeze.

They sip on smoothies made of stars,
Debate the best spots for space cars.
With rocket boots they prance and glide,
In a carnival that won't subside.

Meteors fly like shooting balls,
Playing dodgeball in dusty halls.
Their laughter echoes all around,
In a universe that knows no bounds.

With every bounce, they lose their hats,
Children giggle, chasing friendly cats.
In a romp through red and golden beams,
They live out all their wildest dreams.

Crescendos in the Crimson Desert

In the crimson dunes where shadows play,
Silly creatures dance the day away.
They wear sombreros made of light,
Under the moon that's sparkly bright.

Crickets chirp in perfect time,
As cacti hum their little rhyme.
A waltz with balls of blue and green,
The funniest sight you ever seen.

A cowboy with eight arms leads the way,
Singing tunes where the suns all sway.
With every twirl, a cactus sighs,
In a land where laughter never dies.

They gallop on unicycles mad,
Through this world, oh, they are glad.
As sandstorms swirl in playful jest,
In the desert, they find their rest.

Sonnet of Silent Horizons

On horizons where the sunsets smile,
A funny parade creeps in with style.
Giggling rocks play peek-a-boo,
In shades of pink and vibrant blue.

With telescopes made of jelly beans,
They watch for ships with cotton screens.
Each humor-filled celestial show,
Makes time freeze, while giggles flow.

Oddly shaped clouds do a sly waltz,
As planets engage in silly vaults.
A comet dressed in disco flair,
Whirls around without a care.

In silence, joy can be found,
With laughter echoing all around.
A harmony where weirdness sings,
In spaces vast where happiness clings.

Poems from the Perilous Plains

In the perilous plains where tumbleweeds roam,
Funny critters have made it their home.
They frolic and play, no worries in sight,
Dressed in wild outfits, oh what a sight!

With pogo sticks and a game of tag,
Tentacled friends wagging a flag.
Flying saucers that compete in a race,
Zipping and zooming all over the place.

They share silly stories of far-off lands,
Where space bananas grow in bands.
At night, they gather under a tree,
To share a laugh and drink cosmic tea.

With every sunrise, a grand parade,
Through vibrant valleys that sunshine made.
All in good fun, they celebrate life,
In a world where joy conquers strife.

www.ingramcontent.com/pod-product-compliance
Lightning Source LLC
Chambersburg PA
CBHW051638160426
43209CB00004B/701